Who Was Ida B. Wells?

by Sarah Fabiny

illustrated by Ted Hammond

Penguin Workshop

For all those who crusade for justice—SF

For my kids, Stephanie and Jason—TH

PENGUIN WORKSHOP
An Imprint of Penguin Random House LLC, New York

Visit us online at www.penguinrandomhouse.com.

Library of Congress Control Number: 2019054704

ISBN 9780593093351 (paperback)   10 9 8 7 6 5 4 3 2 1
ISBN 9780593093368 (library binding)   10 9 8 7 6 5 4 3 2 1

Contents

Who Was Ida B. Wells?

Ida B. Wells was born to Elizabeth and James Wells on July 16, 1862. They both were enslaved on a farm in Holly Springs, Mississippi. Because her parents were slaves, that meant Ida was born enslaved, too. But on January 1, 1863, when Ida was less than six months old, President Abraham Lincoln signed the Emancipation Proclamation.

The Civil War between the North and the South was still raging. The proclamation granted freedom to all slaves who lived in Southern states fighting against the North. When the Civil War was finally over in 1865, slavery ended in all of the United States.

Now freed slaves were allowed to attend school. They could learn how to read and write. Before that, teaching enslaved people to read and write had been against the law.

Ida's parents had never been to school. But they knew how important it was for their children to get an education. Ida later said, "Our job was to go to school and learn all we could."

Ida loved school! She got good grades and read every book she could get her hands on. By the time she was six years old, she could read very well.

Ida's father used to invite his friends over to the Wellses' house. The men would talk about all kinds of things, including what it was like to have been enslaved. Ida's father and his friends also discussed how they were still treated badly even though they were now free men. Ida saw that they were often fearful.

Ida's father would often ask Ida to read the newspaper aloud to him and his friends. James was proud that his daughter was able to read so well. He also wanted Ida to see how powerful the written word could be. Ida didn't always understand what the articles meant. Still, newspapers gave her knowledge about the world outside Holly Springs.

Even though she was still quite young, Ida realized that black people didn't have the same rights as white people. It was very hard for black people to get a decent job. In the South, white people made it hard for them to vote. Ida saw that there was injustice in the world around her.

Could she do something to change that?

CHAPTER 1
Freedom

After the Civil War ended, James and Elizabeth Wells chose to stay on the farm where they had always lived. Now the man who owned the farm had to pay them for the work they did.

Ida and her family on the farm where she was born

Ida's parents were able to save money. After several years, they decided to rent their own house in Holly Springs. They wanted to build a new life for themselves and their growing family.

At school, Ida was smart and learned quickly. But she often had a hard time getting along with the other students. She had strong opinions and wasn't afraid to say what was on her mind—even to the teachers.

Rebuilding the South

Much of the South was destroyed during the Civil War and needed to be rebuilt. This period of rebuilding was called Reconstruction. It lasted from 1865 to 1877. The federal government helped the South rebuild roads, farms, and schools. The federal government also wanted to secure the rights of the newly freed slaves. Several amendments (changes) were added to the Constitution during this time:

- Thirteenth Amendment (December 1865): Abolished (ended) slavery everywhere in the United States
- Fourteenth Amendment (July 1868): Gave freed slaves the right of citizenship
- Fifteenth Amendment (February 1870): Granted black men the right to vote

Reconstruction officially ended in 1877 while Rutherford B. Hayes was the president. Each state in the South once again took over running its own government. Many of them ignored the rights that the recently freed black people had gained.

In the summer of 1878, Ida went to visit her grandmother on her farm outside of Holly Springs. While Ida was away, a yellow fever epidemic hit the South. Yellow fever is a disease that is carried by mosquitoes. It is called *yellow fever* because in serious cases, a person's skin turns a yellow color. The disease swept through parts of Mississippi, including Holly Springs. Many people left town, but Ida's family stayed. Her father helped take care of the sick and made coffins for those who had died. Sadly, both Ida's parents and her youngest brother died from the disease.

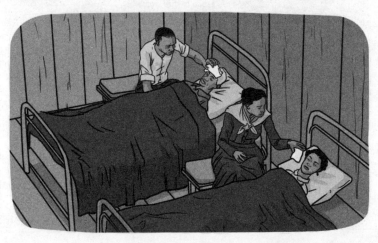

When Ida returned to Holly Springs, friends of her parents were talking about what should happen to the Wells children who had survived. Perhaps they should be split up and sent to live with other families. Ida was shocked by this. She told her parents' friends that it would make her father and mother turn over in their graves to know their children had been scattered, and if they helped Ida find work, she would take care of her brothers and sisters.

At that time, there was a need for black teachers in rural areas out in the countryside. Two of the grown-ups taking care of the Wells children suggested that Ida take the test to become a teacher. If she passed it, then Ida could look after her brothers and sisters. So Ida studied hard, took the test, and passed.

One of her aunts helped lower the hems on Ida's dresses and put up her hair to make her look older. Ida was only sixteen years old. But she made a promise to herself. For the rest of her life, she would never back away from a challenge.

CHAPTER 2
"Princess of the Press"

Every Sunday afternoon, Ida rode a mule to the school where she taught during the week. On Friday nights, she would ride back to Holly Springs. On Saturday and Sunday, Ida did the washing, ironing, and cooking for her younger brothers and sisters. Friends and family looked after Ida's siblings during the days while she was away teaching.

Reconstruction had given most black people equal rights with white people. But white people in the Southern states now began passing new laws to undo this. These new laws were known as Jim Crow laws. They made it hard for black

men to vote. Black children couldn't go to school with white children. They had to go to separate schools, just for black children. Many of these schools were very crowded. They often had no paper, books, or school supplies. This was the kind of school Ida taught in. It was hard to get her students to listen and learn. But Ida did not let this stand in her way.

Jim Crow

The purpose of Jim Crow laws was to keep black people separate from white people. This separation, called segregation, was put in place in schools, restaurants, public restrooms, and on public transportation.

The name *Jim Crow* comes from a black character who was in skits and songs in the late 1820s and early 1830s. The character was lazy and shabbily dressed. He was actually played by a white man who had darkened his skin using burnt cork. Today, the practice of wearing blackface is offensive.

In the South, Jim Crow laws lasted until the middle of the 1900s.

After two years of teaching at the country school, Ida's aunt Fannie invited Ida and her two youngest sisters to move to Memphis, Tennessee. Ida jumped at the chance to leave Mississippi. Teaching in a city school meant she would earn more money and have the materials she needed. And it also meant that Ida, now nineteen, would have some free time for herself.

Ida made new friends in Memphis. She and her friends went to plays and concerts and attended church. She also joined a club called the Lyceum.

The Lyceum had its own newsletter. It was called the *Evening Star*. When the editor moved away, who was chosen to replace him?

Ida!

Ida loved writing and editing the newsletter. On Friday nights, she read it aloud. She was so good that people who weren't members of the Lyceum came to listen to her. Her parents would have been so proud.

One night, a minister came to hear Ida. He was very impressed by her. He asked her to write a column for his weekly newspaper, the *Living Way*. Ida was happy to accept his offer.

Most women who wrote for newspapers at this time wrote about marriage, children, and running a household. But not Ida. She wrote about how badly some white people treated black people.

It was very brave of Ida to write these articles. At that time, not many black people were willing to speak out against the injustice they suffered.

During this time, Ida taught at a school just north of Memphis. She traveled by train to get there. Tennessee had passed a Jim Crow law stating that black and white train passengers must ride in separate cars. Ida decided to ignore the law.

One day in 1884, she bought a first-class ticket and rode in the ladies' car. It was only for white women. When the conductor came by, he told Ida to move to the train car for black people. But Ida refused. She said she had a right to be in the car because she had a first-class ticket. The conductor and two other men dragged Ida out of her seat.

Did that make her move to the other car? No! Instead, Ida got off the train and returned to Memphis. Then she decided to fight back against the railroad. Ida hired a lawyer and went to court.

After several months, a judge decided that the railroad had been wrong. The judge ruled that the railroad pay Ida five hundred dollars to make up for how she had been treated, but she never got the money. Ida was only twenty-one years old and five feet tall. But she had stood up to a powerful company and won.

Ida decided to write about what had happened in her column for the *Living Way*. The article was so popular that other newspapers across the country reprinted it. Ida was becoming known as a brave journalist who wrote about what mattered to black people.

Even though Ida continued to teach, it was writing for newspapers that she enjoyed most. She remembered how she had read the newspaper to her father and his friends. Now it would be Ida's own words that would make a difference.

Soon the owners of a local newspaper called the *Free Speech and Headlight* asked Ida to come work for them. She said she would under one condition—that she become the editor and a part owner of the newspaper. The owners agreed. In 1889, Ida became one of the country's few black female newspaper owners and editors.

Readers liked Ida's writing. Ida said, "I wrote in a plain, common-sense way on the things which concerned our people . . . I never used a word of two syllables where one would serve the purpose." In one column for the *Free Speech and Headlight*, Ida wrote that black people should not always be loyal to one political party over another. That was because Ida believed every political party should fight against racial injustice. In another column, she stated that women could do as much in the world as men. Her practical advice helped people in their daily lives. After a while, her fans gave her the nickname "Princess of the Press."

In 1891, Ida wrote an article about the school system in Memphis. The schools in the city were segregated. Ida's article said that the white people who ran the school system were cheating black children out of a good education. She criticized the "inadequate buildings" where black children went to school. She also claimed that many of the teachers hired to teach black students were not good enough. These were bold and brave things

to say. But, as always, Ida said what she thought. When the article was published, the people in charge of the Memphis school system were very upset. They fired Ida because of the article.

Ida knew her job as a teacher had been important. But maybe being a full-time journalist would mean even more. She could reach a lot of people with her words. And with those words, Ida could get people to join her fight for justice.

CHAPTER 3
The Crusade Begins

Ida enjoyed working at the *Free Speech*. However, for the newspaper to make enough money, more people had to buy it. Ida took the train to towns in Mississippi, Arkansas, and Tennessee to convince people to buy the *Free Speech*. In less than a year, subscriptions went from 1,500 to 4,000.

It was while Ida was on one of these trips that she received some horrible news. Three black men in Memphis had been killed. One of the men was named Thomas Moss. He had been Ida's good friend. Thomas was a letter carrier, and he delivered the mail to the *Free Speech* office. He often heard news while on his delivery route, and he shared it with Ida so that she could scoop other papers. (To *scoop* means to get a news story out first.) Ida rushed back to Memphis to find out what had happened.

Thomas Moss

Thomas Moss and two other black men, Calvin McDowell and Henry Steward, had run a store called the Peoples Grocery. It was very successful. That made many white people angry,

especially a man named William Barrett. William owned a grocery store right across the street. He felt that business was being taken away from him. He organized a mob of people to ruin the Peoples Grocery. Thomas and his friends knew that the Memphis police would not help them. The three black men would have to defend their store themselves.

When the mob attacked, Thomas and his friends fired their guns to scare off everyone.

Three white men were injured. The rest ran away. The next day, none of the white men in the mob were arrested. However, Thomas and his friends were put in jail. They hoped that in court, a judge would understand that they had been protecting their store. But Thomas and his friends never got to court. A mob of white men took them from their jail cell and killed them. When someone is killed like this without a trial, it is called *lynching*.

Charles Lynch and Lynching

The terms *lynching* and *lynch law* were named for Colonel Charles Lynch. During the Revolutionary War, he created his own court that punished people who remained loyal to England.

Up until the Civil War, lynch mobs out in rural areas usually went after common criminals—both white and black—such as horse thieves. But after the Civil War and Reconstruction, lynching happened mainly to black people in the South. Most often, they were hanged from a tree and left for others to see. Lynchings were warnings to other black people to stay in their place. From 1882 to 1900, 2,858 people were lynched in the United States—1,107 white people and 1,751 black people.

only one thing we can do: Save our money and leave a town which will neither protect our lives and property, nor give us a fair trial in the courts.

What did Ida do about these terrible murders? She wrote an article. A few days after the lynching, Ida's article appeared in *Free Speech*. Ida used strong words in her article. She told the black people of Memphis that there was "only one thing we can do: Save our money and leave a town which will neither protect our lives and property, nor give us a fair trial in the courts . . ."

Many black citizens in Memphis listened to Ida and left. And many black people who stayed refused to ride the city streetcars or shop at stores owned by white people. On her own, Ida had started one of the first boycotts in the United States. (A boycott is a type of protest in which people refuse to do business with a company.)

Thomas Moss had been a very honest, hardworking, and innocent man. How many other innocent people had also been lynched? Ida decided to find out.

She traveled to towns in the South to talk to black people about what they had seen or heard. As she suspected, many who had been lynched were not guilty of a crime. She was shocked to learn that sometimes newspapers encouraged lynchings.

The more Ida learned about lynching, the angrier she got. She had already written an article about Thomas Moss. But here was a much bigger issue. In May 1892, Ida wrote an article about everything she had found out about lynching.

Afterward, Ida headed to New York City. She had been invited there by T. Thomas Fortune. He was the editor of the leading black newspaper in the country. It was called the *New York Age*. He was impressed by Ida's writing, and the newspaper had reprinted many of her articles.

T. Thomas Fortune

T. Thomas Fortune met Ida at the train station when she arrived in Jersey City. "Well," he said, "we've been a long time getting you to New York, but now that you are here, I am afraid that you'll have to stay." Then T. Thomas Fortune showed her a copy of the *New York Sun* newspaper. It had a story about the *Free Speech* offices in Memphis.

Ida's article about lynching had made many white people in Memphis so angry that they broke into the *Free Speech* offices. Then they destroyed the printing press. They also left a note for Ida saying they would lynch her if she ever tried to publish the newspaper again.

Ida realized she could not go back to Memphis. But what would she do now? T. Thomas Fortune came up with a solution—Ida could move to New York City and work at the *New York Age*. Ida accepted his offer. Her new life in the North was about to begin.

CHAPTER 4
Speaking Farther and Wider

Fortunately, Ida had all the notes she had taken about lynching. She used them to write an article for the *New York Age*. The article was published on June 25, 1892. T. Thomas Fortune printed ten thousand copies and they all sold.

Ida was thrilled. Her message about the horrors of lynching was reaching more and more people.

One of those people was Frederick Douglass. He was a well-known black leader. Ida's article had opened his eyes to the horrible crime. Douglass suggested that Ida write a pamphlet—a longer, more detailed piece—about lynching. Ida agreed. The title of the pamphlet was *Southern Horrors: Lynch Law in All Its Phases*. But how would Ida pay for the pamphlet to get published?

Two women helped organize a speaking event for Ida. The money raised would help her pay for the pamphlet. The event, held at New York City's Lyric Hall, was a success. After that, Ida started receiving invitations to speak to other groups.

Frederick Douglass (1818–1895)

Frederick Douglass is one of the most famous black leaders in US history. He was born enslaved in 1818. Even though it was against the law, the wife of his master taught him the alphabet. From there, Frederick taught himself to read and write. Then he taught other enslaved people how to read, using the Bible.

Over the next several years, Frederick tried to escape to the North. He was finally successful in 1838. Frederick made his way to New York, and he eventually settled in Massachusetts. Soon, he began speaking to groups about abolishing slavery. He became well known for his passionate and inspiring speeches.

During the Civil War, Frederick became an adviser to President Abraham Lincoln. Throughout Reconstruction he fought for the rights of former slaves. He also became a supporter of the women's right-to-vote movement.

Frederick Douglass continued to be an activist, speaker, and writer until he died in 1895 at the age of seventy-seven.

Ida spoke in Massachusetts, Rhode Island, Delaware, Pennsylvania, and Washington, DC. Sometimes the groups were just black people. But she also spoke to audiences of white people.

Ida was surprised but happy that many white people wanted to join her antilynching crusade. (A crusade is a fight against something considered evil.)

Catherine Impey

In 1893, Ida got a chance to take her message farther. She received an invitation to speak in England. The invitation was from Catherine Impey, a white Englishwoman who had met Ida in Philadelphia. Catherine and a friend had formed a group against racial segregation.

Ida hoped that speaking in England might help her cause in the United States. Americans were influenced by opinions and trends in England. If Ida could get the English to support her antilynching campaign, perhaps the US government would do something at home.

Ida spoke at public meetings, clubs, and churches throughout England and Scotland. She was interviewed by reporters. One newspaper said "freedom is mocked in the country that boasts herself the freest in the world."

Ferdinand Barnett

Ida returned to the United States in June 1893. But she didn't go home to New York City. Instead, she headed to Chicago to join a group of black leaders at the world's fair. The group included Frederick Douglass and Ferdinand Barnett, a black lawyer who was publisher of Chicago's first black newspaper, the *Conservator*.

The world's fair was celebrating the four hundredth anniversary of Christopher Columbus's voyage to the New World in 1492. The fair had many exhibits that showed all the progress the world had made since then. However, none of the US exhibits included black people. The group of black leaders was there to protest this.

Chicago World's Fair, 1893

While she was in Chicago, Ida visited black churches, where she spoke about lynching and segregation. She came to love the city. Many black people lived there. They were an active part of life in the city. And they were interested in her antilynching crusade. So instead of going back to New York City, Ida decided to stay in Chicago.

Ida accepted an offer from Ferdinand Barnett to work part-time for the *Conservator*. Ida also decided to organize a group for black women in the city. It was the first black women's club in Chicago.

Chicago appealed to Ida for another reason: Ferdinand Barnett himself.

Ida was in love. She and Ferdinand were very different, but they were a good match. Many years later, Ida's granddaughter explained that "in an era when most men expected women to stay at home and not speak out on social issues, Ferdinand accepted the fact that Ida was an activist and encouraged her in her work." Ida knew that Ferdinand was the kind of man she wanted to spend her life with.

CHAPTER 5
Braver and Bolder

Ida and Ferdinand didn't get married right away. Ida was too busy working. She was writing a book called *A Red Record*. Ida gave it that title because the book described some of the bloodiest lynchings. Then, after a second trip to England, Ida went straight out on another US speaking tour. In Rochester, New York, she was invited to stay at the home of Susan B. Anthony. Susan was the leader of the fight for women's suffrage (the right to vote). That, too, became an important cause for Ida.

Susan B. Anthony

A year later, Ida returned to Chicago. In June 1895, she published *A Red Record*. Besides describing lynchings, the book included photographs. They were difficult to look at. But they showed people just how horrible lynching was.

That same month, on June 27, Ida and Ferdinand were finally married. Ida decided to hyphenate her name to Ida B. Wells-Barnett. While this is common today, at the time it was very unusual. In March 1896, Ida gave birth to a son named Charles. People had been surprised that Ida had married. They were even more surprised when she had a baby. Many people were sure that having a baby would mean that Ida would give up her work. But they were wrong. She brought Charles to the office, and she took him to meetings and conferences. After her second son, Herman, was born in November 1897, Ida briefly tried focusing just on her family. But three months later, a lynching in South Carolina brought Ida back to work.

The black man who had been killed was an employee of the US government.

The US government needed to take action.

An antilynching group in Chicago raised money to send someone to Washington, DC, to speak with President William McKinley.

The person chosen was Ida.

Ida meets with President William McKinley, 1898

The president listened to Ida. He promised to track down and punish the men who had carried out the lynching. But sadly, that didn't happen. Shortly after Ida's visit, the United States went to war with Spain. The president was focused on the war. Little was done to bring the lynch mob to justice. Once again, Ida felt let down by people in power.

This was not a promising time for civil rights in the United States. A couple of years earlier, the Supreme Court had ruled that racial segregation was legal. T. Thomas Fortune wanted to fight this decision, and he wanted Ida to help him. He started to form a new group, the National Afro-American Council. Ida thought maybe this group would get the US government to do something. So she agreed to help.

However, another group of black leaders was willing to go along with the court's decision. They felt that by agreeing to segregation, they

A separate fountain for black people

could keep the peace. The group believed white people would respect and accept black people if they worked hard and got an education, but kept themselves separate. This group was led by a man named Booker T. Washington.

It upset Ida that some black leaders felt black people had to earn the approval of white people. When the National Afro-American Council met in Washington, DC, Ida gave a speech. She criticized Booker T. Washington for agreeing to segregation. Ida said, "If this gathering means anything, it means that we have at last come to a point where we must do something for ourselves—and do it now." People at the meeting called Ida a "hothead" and booed her.

It was hard knowing that a large group of black people didn't support her approach to equality. However, it made Ida more determined than ever to continue her fight. Even if that meant making more enemies. Not just with white people. But with black people, too.

Separate but Equal

The state of Louisiana had a law saying that white people and black people must ride in different cars on trains, but required the train cars be "equal." Homer Plessy,

Homer Plessy

who was one-eighth black, was arrested for riding in a whites-only car. He challenged the Louisiana law, saying it was against the US Constitution. But in 1896, the US Supreme Court—the highest court in the United States—ruled in the case called *Plessy v. Ferguson* that segregation was legal, as long as equally good facilities, such as train cars, public restrooms, and water fountains, were provided for both races.

In 1954, the US Supreme Court partially overturned this "separate but equal" ruling. In *Brown v. Board of Education*, the court made it illegal to segregate schools by race. This was the beginning of the end of Jim Crow laws.

Booker T. Washington (1856–1915)

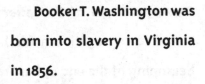

Booker T. Washington was born into slavery in Virginia in 1856.

In 1881, when he was just twenty-five years old, Booker was asked to be the head of a new school for black students, the Tuskegee Normal and Industrial Institute (now known as the Tuskegee Institute). While he was there, Tuskegee became one of the leading schools in the United States. Washington thought that by getting an education, black people would have the ability to get better jobs and earn decent money. He believed this was more important than voting rights or political rights. Washington thought if black people were patient, they would eventually gain acceptance and respect from white people.

CHAPTER 6
Never Give Up

In the late 1890s, Ida wrote more pamphlets about lynchings. More people became aware of what was happening. And, indeed, the number of lynchings was decreasing. But Ida was frustrated that the federal government still would not pass an antilynching law.

In 1900, Ida decided to fight a battle closer
to home. The *Chicago Tribune* had run several
articles about changing the city's school system,
which put black and white students together.
Many white people wanted the city's schools to be
segregated, just as in the South. Ida felt this was
wrong and unjust. She wrote a letter to the editor
of the newspaper. She asked him to meet with a
group of black leaders. When Ida did not get a
reply to her letter, she went to the newspaper's
office. The editor claimed he did not have time to
listen to her argument.

Ida was not going to give up, but she knew she would need help. And she knew exactly who could help her—a woman named Jane Addams. Jane Addams had founded Hull House. Hull House was in Chicago. It helped people in need with food, housing, and education. Jane Addams was respected by the people of Chicago. And because education was so important to Jane Addams, she agreed to help Ida. She got a group of people to go speak to the *Chicago Tribune*. And this time, the newspaper agreed to stop publishing articles calling for segregated schools.

Hull House

Jane Addams (1860–1935)

As a young girl, Jane Addams knew that when she grew up, she wanted to help people who were not as fortunate as she was.

In 1889, Jane and a friend opened Hull House in a poor neighborhood in Chicago. It was named after the first owners of the house and was open to immigrants who had come to the city to find work and make a better life. Hull House offered day care for young children, a club for teenage boys, and sewing and cooking lessons for girls. It also provided art, music, and citizenship classes for adults. Through Hull House, Jane Addams helped people find jobs and adjust to life in the United States. But she also gave them the opportunity to relax and enjoy life.

In 1901, Ida gave birth to her third child, a little girl named Ida Jr. And three years later, another girl, Alfreda, was born. Ida now had four children to look after. The Wells-Barnett house was a busy one! Family was important to Ida and Ferdinand, but Ida never wanted to give up the work she did. Ida still found time to write and travel to give speeches about her antilynching crusade.

In 1909, Ida and a group of people, both black and white, established an organization called the National Association for the Advancement of Colored People—the NAACP. It would work to put an end to lynching and segregation.

Some members of the NAACP, however, felt that Ida and her ideas were too harsh. A

Founding members of the NAACP

man named W. E. B. Du Bois had become a prominent voice among black leaders. He believed her ideas made the fight for the rights of black people more difficult. He did not want Ida to be one of the NAACP's leaders. Also, most people involved in the new group were men. They simply did not want a woman to have as much power as they

W. E. B. Du Bois

did. Ida became frustrated with the NAACP and eventually stopped working with them. She felt that they were too cautious. She thought they were more concerned with helping wealthy black people than with uplifting the poor and powerless.

The NAACP ignored Ida and all the work she had done. But did that stop her? Of course not!

Toward the end of 1909, a man was lynched in Cairo, Illinois. The sheriff did nothing to stop the mob of white people. But in Illinois, a law said a sheriff would lose his job if he didn't do all he could to prevent a lynching. So the governor of Illinois removed the sheriff.

There was a catch, however. The law also allowed a sheriff to ask the governor for his job back.

Ida was afraid the governor would agree to do that.

NAACP

In 1908, a race riot took place in Springfield, Illinois—the hometown of Abraham Lincoln. There needed to be a national organization to fight against injustice toward black people. So in 1909, a group founded the NAACP to mark the one hundredth anniversary of Lincoln's birth. They wanted to honor the president who had done the most to end slavery in the United States. The NAACP's mission was to work to eliminate racism. It wanted to abolish segregation and discrimination in the workplace, in schools, and on public transportation. It also wanted to put an end to lynching.

The NAACP grew through the early 1900s and gained national attention during the civil rights movement in the 1950s and 1960s. The organization supported the work of Martin Luther King Jr. and other black activists.

Today, the NAACP is the country's largest and most recognized civil rights organization. It continues to fight to end racism, but it also works to get young black people to register to vote, get involved with their communities, and run for public office.

Ida knew that someone needed to be at court in Cairo, Illinois, to make sure that didn't happen. But she was not a lawyer, and she was busy at home looking after her children and writing. Finally, her son Charles, who was thirteen, said to her, "Mother, if you don't go, nobody else will!" So Ida got on a train and traveled to Cairo.

In the courtroom, Ida spoke her words with passion and feeling. If the sheriff was allowed to

go back to work, it would send the wrong message to the people in Illinois and across the country. Ida asked that the governor do the right thing and not give the sheriff his job back.

Ida went home and waited for the governor's decision. Finally, he gave his verdict: The sheriff would not get his job back. "Mob violence has no place in Illinois," the governor said. Ida's words had won. An antilynching law had been upheld. It was a clear warning to lynch mobs.

CHAPTER 7
New Crusades

Ida was always looking for ways to help black people. Many young black men had moved to Chicago from the South in the early 1900s. Ida wanted to give them a place to stay and help them find work. So in 1908, she established the Negro Fellowship League. It was similar to her friend Jane Addams's Hull House. It was a neighborhood center in a poor part of Chicago. At the Negro Fellowship League, young black men were able to get a room and hot meals, use the library, and get help finding a job.

At the end of the first year, Ida and the staff had found jobs for 115 young men. And about 45 men stayed there each night. Ida was proud of her neighborhood project. A wealthy

newspaper publisher and his wife had given Ida the money to start the project. They were proud, too, of what she was doing. They gave her more money so that the Negro Fellowship League could stay open for two more years. After that, however, their support ended.

So Ida did what she always did—she kept on going. She moved the center to a smaller space that was less expensive. That would help keep the center open. Ida became Chicago's first female probation officer. A probation officer works with the courts to help people who have been released from jail lead a good life.

The job as a probation officer was hard work. Ida was on duty at the courthouse every day from nine in the morning to twelve noon. Once she was done there, she traveled around the city to check up on the eighty-five men who were on probation. And then she would head to the Negro Fellowship League. Ida often made sure that many of the men she looked after at the courthouse came to the Negro Fellowship League. That helped them stay out of trouble.

Ida also wanted to help black women in the

city. She realized that black women in Chicago and the United States would never get certain opportunities unless they were able to vote. So Ida decided to get involved in the suffrage movement. In January 1913, with the assistance of two suffragists, she formed the Alpha Suffrage Club. It was the first voting rights organization for black women in Illinois. The club met every week at the Negro Fellowship League.

Alpha Suffrage Club members

Ida was now fifty years old. She was no longer a young woman, but she gave no thought to slowing down. She was working as a probation officer, running the Negro Fellowship League and the Alpha Suffrage Club, editing a newsletter and a newspaper, going to meetings, writing articles, and looking after her family. For Ida, there was always more work to be done.

In 1913, five thousand women from all across the United States organized a march that would take place in Washington, DC. The marchers wanted Woodrow Wilson, the new president, to push for women's right to vote. Ida traveled to Washington, DC, with the Alpha Suffrage Club to join the march.

Did all these women, black and white, unite behind their shared goal?

Woodrow Wilson

Ida at the 1913 Woman Suffrage Parade in Washington, DC

That was what Ida hoped for. But the white
women in a group from Illinois asked Ida and
the black women with her to march separately!
At the back of the parade! They were afraid that
suffragists from the South would not want to see
black women marching with white women.

Ida couldn't believe it. This was against everything that she had been fighting for. She was not going to be kept separate. Ida said, "If we don't stand by our principles, the parade will be a farce." (A farce is a joke.) So she joined the white women. Ida didn't care if it upset anyone.

However, President Wilson was not concerned with the voting rights of women, whether black or white, at that time. He was more concerned about keeping the United States out of World War I.

That didn't happen. In 1917, more than two million US soldiers went overseas to fight in the war. Four hundred thousand of those soldiers were black. Their efforts helped win the war for the Allied powers. They served their country bravely. The black soldiers felt they had contributed as much as white soldiers. On their return home, they expected to be treated with respect and have the same opportunities as white men. Plus, being in the armed services had taught black soldiers how to fight back when attacked.

Many white people resented the attitude of the returning black soldiers. They wanted them kept in their place. Tension between groups of black people and white people grew.

African American troops arriving in France,
during World War I, 1917

World War I (1914–1918)

World War I, or the Great War, as it was called at the time, started in 1914. Europe had split into two alliances, or sides. One alliance, called the Allied powers, was made up of Great Britain, France, and Russia. The other alliance, called the Central powers,

German submarines attacked US merchant ships, 1916

included Germany, Austria-Hungary, and Turkey.

President Wilson managed to keep the United States out of the war for a long time. But early in 1917, German submarines attacked US merchant ships. So, finally, on April 6, 1917, the United States declared war on Germany. The US entry into the war helped the Allied powers win World War I.

In the summer of 1919, things exploded. There were riots in many towns and cities across the United States, including Chicago. Ferdinand and the children stayed inside during the riots.

Chicago race riot, 1919

But Ida went to the neighborhood where they were occuring. Like always, she talked to people and tried to find out exactly what was happening.

Ida submitted a report to the city officials in Chicago. She hoped that the city would punish the white gangs who had started the riots. She also wanted city officials to stop segregation. The city officials listened but did nothing. Once again, Ida felt like she was fighting on her own, and that no one else cared about changing the world.

CHAPTER 8
Ups and Downs

The riots in the summer of 1919 were a blow to Ida. She felt like her antilynching work wasn't making a difference. But there was good news coming.

American women had helped greatly with the war effort. President Wilson recognized that it was time for women to have the right to vote.

US women cheer after getting the right to vote

And in June 1919, the US Congress approved an amendment to the Constitution that would allow women to vote. The amendment was passed on August 18, 1920. Ida's work for the suffrage movement had gotten results!

Unfortunately, that same year, Ida was forced to close the Negro Fellowship League. Although the organization had provided aid to ten thousand men, women, and children, it simply became too costly for her to keep the place running. One week after the Negro Fellowship League closed, Ida became ill and had to have an operation.

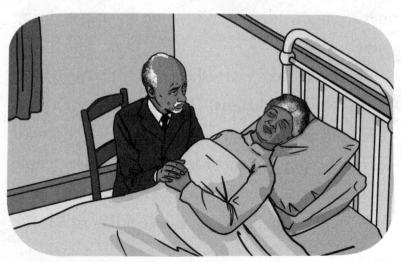

Problems set in afterward, and for a while it looked like Ida might not survive. After five weeks in the hospital, the doctors allowed her to go home. But she soon had to return to the hospital and was there for another eight weeks. It took her almost a year to completely recover.

Ida's husband and children wanted her to stop working so hard. She had been fighting for equality and justice since she had been pulled off a train when she was just twenty-one years old. But even though her illness had sapped her strength, Ida was not going to stop fighting now.

In 1922, Ida was asked to visit a prison in Little Rock, Arkansas. Twelve black men had been put in jail. They had been wrongly accused of planning a riot in order to hurt white people and take their land. Although innocent, they had been sentenced to death. Ida asked the men to give their side of the story. She made sure she got as much information as possible from them.

When Ida returned to Chicago, she used her notes to write a pamphlet called *The Arkansas Race Riot*. It told how white farmers had cheated the twelve men out of money they had earned. The pamphlet also stated that the men only confessed to a crime because they were beaten and tortured.

And it described how the trial had been unfair. What Ida wanted was a new trial for the men. She had the pamphlet printed, and she sent it to important people in Arkansas.

Ida's pamphlet drew a lot of attention. The case went all the way to the Supreme Court. And in 1923, the judges ruled that the twelve men had been treated unjustly and had not received a fair trial. All of them were set free.

It was a great victory for the men—and for Ida as well.

Ida was in her sixties now. Her husband and children were worried about her health, but it was impossible to make her slow down. She began to work on the story of her life. And in 1930, at the age of sixty-eight, Ida announced that she was going to run for a senate seat in the Illinois state government. There were several black men in office in Illinois at that time. However, Ida didn't think they were doing enough to support the rights of black people.

Ida did not do well in the election. She got

only 762 votes, while the winner received 4,502. But Ida was proud that she had at least tried. She hoped other black women would follow in her path.

On a Saturday in March, Ida went shopping. She came home earlier than expected, saying she didn't feel well. She stayed in bed the next day, skipping church and a visit to her sister Annie. Ida's family realized she must be very sick, so they took her to the hospital. It was kidney disease, the doctors said. And there was nothing to be done. Ida died a few days later on March 25, 1931, four months before her sixty-ninth birthday.

Over the course of her life, there were many times when Ida felt she was not making enough of a difference. Yet at her funeral, the church was packed. Many people stood outside, simply wanting to pay their last respects. To show their gratitude.

Getting Results

Ida started her antilynching campaign in 1892, and she continued her crusade until she died. Even though she felt that not enough was being done, her tireless work and writing brought the problem to the attention of people in the United States and around the world. The number of lynchings in the country went down each decade that she carried on her crusade.

1885:   184 lynchings in the United States

1895:   179 lynchings in the United States

1905:   62 lynchings in the United States

1914:   55 lynchings in the United States

1925:   17 lynchings in the United States

These days, lynching is rare in the United States, but it does still happen.

For instance, in 1998, three white men in Texas killed James Byrd Jr. by dragging him behind a pickup truck for three miles. In this case, all of the men went to trial and were found guilty,

James Byrd Jr.

with two of the three getting the death penalty.

CHAPTER 9
"Eternal Vigilance Is the Price of Liberty"

Ida used the phrase "Eternal Vigilance Is the Price of Liberty" in the last chapter of her autobiography, *Crusade for Justice*. The saying

means that people who want the benefits of freedom must work hard and never take those rights for granted. Ida B. Wells is certainly an example of that. She worked tirelessly her whole life to gain liberty, freedom, and justice for herself and all black people.

After her death, Ida's work was not fully recognized. However, that changed once the civil rights and women's rights movements began in the 1950s and 1960s. More and more people learned about Ida B. Wells and all that she had accomplished. She was one of the country's first activists for the rights of black people. She had been brave and fearless, and she never backed down from a fight. Ida's courage paved the way for black activists such as Rosa Parks, Martin Luther King Jr., Medgar Evers, and Shirley Chisholm.

Martin Luther King Jr. and Shirley Chisholm

As for her autobiography, Ida never finished it. The last chapter actually stopped in the middle of a sentence. But Ida's daughter wanted the world to hear her mother's story. The autobiography was published in 1970. In 1990, the US Postal Service honored Ida with a stamp.

An area at the National Memorial for Peace and Justice in Montgomery, Alabama, is named for her. And the city of Chicago named a major street after her in 2019. It was the first time the city had ever named a street after a black woman. Ida B. Wells's crusade for justice is now seen for what it is—an important part of US history.

National Memorial for Peace and Justice

On April 26, 2018, the National Memorial for Peace and Justice opened in Montgomery, Alabama. It is the first memorial dedicated to the thousands of people who were lynched in the United States. The memorial is made up of 816 rusted steel slabs.

Each slab represents a county in the United States where a lynching took place. The slab contains the names of the black people who were lynched.

The entire memorial is a reminder of slavery, racial segregation, and Jim Crow laws. It is also a reminder of the people, including Ida B. Wells, who fought against these horrible things.

Timeline of Ida B. Wells's Life

1862	Born in Holly Springs, Mississippi, on July 16
1878	Ida takes on responsibility of looking after her siblings
1881	Moves to Memphis
1884	Starts writing a weekly column for the *Living Way*
	Sues the Chesapeake & Ohio railroad company
1889	Becomes part owner and editor of the *Free Speech and Headlight*
1891	Dismissed from job as teacher in Memphis school system
1892	Begins investigating lynchings in the United States
	Publishes *Southern Horrors: Lynch Law in All Its Phases*
1893	Invited to England and Scotland to speak about her antilynching campaign
	Moves to Chicago
1895	Marries Ferdinand L. Barnett
	Publishes *A Red Record*
1909	Helps establish the organization that becomes the National Association for the Advancement of Colored People
1913	Establishes a black women's suffrage organization
1930	Loses election for seat in the Illinois state senate
1931	Dies in Chicago on March 25 at the age of sixty-eight
1990	Ida B. Wells commemorative stamp is issued

Timeline of the World

1833 — Slavery is abolished throughout the British Empire

1852 — *Uncle Tom's Cabin* by Harriet Beecher Stowe is published

1861 — American Civil War begins

1865 — American Civil War ends

1872 — Yellowstone National Park is established

1881 — Tuskegee Normal and Industrial Institute opens in Alabama

1889 — Eiffel Tower is completed

1898 — Spanish-American War

1900 — *The Wonderful Wizard of Oz* by L. Frank Baum is published

1903 — Ford Motor Company is formed

1917 — United States enters World War I

1920 — Women given the right to vote in the United States

1929 — Stock market crash marks beginning of the Great Depression

1932 — Amelia Earhart flies solo across the Atlantic Ocean

1955 — Rosa Parks refuses to give up her seat in the white section of a bus in Montgomery, Alabama

1964 — Civil Rights Act passes

1965 — Voting Rights Act passes

1968 — Shirley Chisholm becomes first black woman elected to Congress

Bibliography

*Books for young readers

Bay, Mia. *To Tell the Truth Freely: The Life of Ida B. Wells.* New York: Hill and Wang, 2009.

*Dray, Philip. *Yours for Justice, Ida B. Wells: The Daring Life of a Crusading Journalist.* Atlanta: Peachtree Publishers, 2008.

*Fradin, Dennis Brindell, and Judith Bloom Fradin. *Ida B. Wells: Mother of the Civil Rights Movement.* New York: Clarion Books, 2000.

Giddings, Paula J. *Ida: A Sword Among Lions: Ida B. Wells and the Campaign Against Lynching.* New York: Amistad, 2008.

*Myers, Walter Dean. *Ida B. Wells: Let the Truth Be Told.* New York: Amistad, 2008.

*Welch, Catherine A., *Ida B. Wells-Barnett: Powerhouse with a Pen.* Minneapolis: Carolrhoda Books, 2000.

Wells, Ida B. *Crusade for Justice: The Autobiography of Ida B. Wells*, edited by Alfreda M. Duster. Chicago: The University of Chicago Press, 1970.

Wells, Ida B. *Southern Horrors and Other Writings: The Anti-Lynching Campaign of Ida B. Wells, 1892–1900*, edited by Jacqueline Jones Royster. Boston: Bedford Books, 1997.

Wells, Ida B. *The Light of Truth: Writings of an Anti-Lynching Crusader*, edited by Mia Bay; general editor, Henry Louis Gates, Jr. New York: Penguin Books, 2014.